Meditation For Beginners

Simple Meditation Techniques To Be Happy And Relieve Stress And Anxiety Forever

Table of Contents

Introduction

I want to thank you and congratulate you for downloading the book, "Meditation-Meditation for Beginners-Simple Meditation Techniques to be Happy and Relieve Stress and Anxiety forever."

This book has lots of actionable information on meditation techniques that can help you to relieve stress and anxiety for good and unleash an era of peace and happiness. I have taken into account that this may be something new to you and have thus included instructions that will help you with your meditation practice as a beginner. This means that you are taught the correct pose, you are also taught how to breathe in a manner that helps you to meditate effectively and also taught how to empty the mind and let go of excess thoughts.

A.C Bhaktivedanta Swami said; ***"You should not be carried away by the dictation of the mind, but the mind should be carried by your dictation."***

Life is tough and a lot of stress and anxiety makes it harder to live. Zen Buddhists put it this way: "Life is full of suffering!" When you think about it critically, a lot of this stress and anxiety comes from being dictated to by your mind and not controlling it.

Let me explain this when you let your emotions and temptations override your conscious mind, and you often do things that aren't beneficial for you, which in turn causes stress.

So how can you take charge? Well, to make your mind listen and do what you want from life, you need to control it and this is where meditation comes in. It not only makes you have total control over your mind but also brings in peace within your soul which makes you feel alive and happy.

This book is designed to help you meditate. It contains actionable techniques that help you meditate easily and get relief from all the stress you have in life. And as the Zen Buddhists put it, while life is full of suffering, there is an end to suffering. My goal in this book is to put an end to suffering by learning the ins and outs of meditation.

Before implementing anything into your life, it is important to have a full understanding of what it is and what it entails. Meditation is no different; before you can learn how to use it to fight stress, anxiety, depression and lots of other problems, it is critical that you know what it is all about.

Chapter One: Meditation: A Comprehensive Understanding

Although meditation is incredibly popular these days, very few people actually understand what it is. Many believe meditation is a way of concentrating on their thoughts alone or imagining something that gives them satisfaction or peace. This is partially true, but this definition doesn't truly define meditation. The purpose of meditation is not to just focus on the mind or thinking of something to make you feel relaxed. It has a purpose that is far higher than these things which bring us to the question; 'What is meditation?'

What is Meditation?

Meditation simply refers to the mental state of thoughtless awareness. This essentially means you are actually meditating if you are aware of everything going on in your mind and around you without thinking or concentrating on that particular situation.

While it is hard to absorb everything going around and within us all the time (we have tens of thousands of internal and external stimuli every single day), in different cultures, numerous techniques are developed to guide people to reach this state of mental awareness.

If meditation is just a state of mind rather than an exercise that makes you think of something calming then how does it help you to relieve your stress and anxiety? Let me explain that:

How Meditation Helps Reduce Stress and Anxiety

As I stated above, meditation is a state of mental and physical awareness. This means that if you are in this state, then you can feel/experience everything that is going in your mind and your surroundings. Therefore, you feel or experience everything that is causing you stress and making you anxious. As you are aware of yourself and surroundings, you detach yourself from the stress-triggering thoughts and circumstances and consequently get rid of the stress and anxiety.

Let me elaborate on that with an example.

Imagine you have been bullied throughout your whole life in school or by an elder brother or another family member. Since you have never received respect, you yearn for it and want everyone to love and respect you. Now you are at the stage of life where you have a job that you don't like and on top of that, a horrible boss. You are not getting respect at the office and this stresses you. Think of this situation and try to imagine yourself in it. Then let's find out how you'd react to it: when you are mentally aware and when you aren't mentally aware.

Case 1: You are not aware of your thoughts and surroundings. You don't know why your boss keeps shouting at you and why you feel stressed all the time. Therefore, you don't know what is it actually that you need to change in order to get your boss' respect. As a result, you just wing it; you keep repeating the same mistakes over and over again, which makes you lose respect the more with each passing day. Ultimately, you are likely to have greater levels of stress.

Case 2: You are aware of your thoughts and surroundings. You know that your mind is craving for respect. You are aware that your boss is shouting at you every day because he/she wants to see daily reports of the project he/she assigned you and you keep trying to avoid him because you are behind schedule. You feel the pressure of not meeting deadlines and this makes you feel stressed, which in turn affects your productivity negatively.

Since you are aware of the situation and the reason why you are stressed, you detach yourself from the situation through meditation and do your work without the fear of not beating the deadline. This increases your productivity and ultimately, you catch up with the schedule and start presenting daily reports to your boss. As a result, your boss starts respecting you again, as you are doing what he/she expects you to do and you are at peace as you are getting what you want: respect from others.

Basically, meditation increases your state of awareness and makes you conscious of things going around you, so you do what's important and discard the meaningless things from your life to become happy and content.

Well, you might easily assume that all this is simple logic but the truth is that meditation has been proven scientifically to help combat stress, anxiety and depression. Let me explain that before we start discussing how to actually meditate for stress and anxiety relief:

In one study[1]
http://www.sciencedaily.com/releases/2013/03/130315095916.htm
participants who meditated were noticed to have greater ability to handle various stressful multitasking tasks as compared to those who never meditated. Meditation does this by initiating different changes in your brain. For instance, whenever you meditate, your frontal lobe (part of

the brain involved in reasoning, planning, emotional control and self-conscious awareness) tends to go offline, which essentially means you are less critical of yourself.

That's not all; meditation can lower the flow of data into your thalamus thus resulting in reduced alertness, which means you are less responsive to external stimuli. Moreover, through meditation, you can increase your focus on creating as well as strengthening such virtues as compassion. To add on, some types of meditation help reduce the density of grey matter in the areas of the brain that are responsible for stress and anxiety, which in turn means you are likely to be less responsive to stress and anxiety triggers.

The thing is; through meditation, you can notice increased focus and greater ability to ignore distractions. To prove that, scientists collected data using functional magnetic resonance imaging (**fMRI** - https://en.m.wikipedia.org/wiki/FMRI) and the results were astonishing; those who meditated noticed a relaxed default mode network - https://en.wikipedia.org/wiki/Default_mode_network. To help you to understand the concept of fMRI, we will briefly talk about the brain regions that are activated when you are at rest/relaxed because this is often associated with reduced anxiety and improved focus. When you meditate, you increase alpha rhythms, which are often connected to creativity, learning, relaxation and great focus. The brain uses many neurons, which usually uses electrical energy to communicate to each other and ultimately create a pretty harmonized network that is linked to a certain state of consciousness. It is through the synchronized electrical connection that brain waves come into existence; such medical equipment like an electroencephalogram (EEG) measures these brainwaves.

The brainwaves exist in different frequencies (5 to be specific), i.e., alpha, beta, delta, theta and gamma and these affect you in various ways. For instance, if you are fully alert and awake, the active brainwave is beta. This helps you to direct your attention to problem solving and decision making. Well, the problem with this statement is that staying in this state for too long is bad for you because it can cause stress and anxiety given that often, logic and critical reasoning can trigger an endless stream of negative thinking pattern, which could even cause mental disorders.

Of the 5 brainwaves, the most useful one for relaxation and treating stress, depression and anxiety is the alpha brainwave. And the good news is that meditation can easily help you to get to this brainwave such that you lower sensory inputs and clear your mind of unwanted thoughts. In simple terms, the alpha brainwaves can help you to focus on one specific thought as opposed to having an endless stream of thoughts. In this state, your brain has increased awareness along with greater focus, which means your mind is likely to focus on certain stimulus for a certain duration of time and as a result, this can help you to apply various positive feelings, which can help you to overcome negative thoughts.

Now that you have learnt how meditation can help you reduce your stress and anxiety levels (by getting you in the alpha brainwave) let's move on and learn some of the techniques to perform meditation. The first one is 'concentration meditation,' which I will discuss in the next chapter.

Chapter Two: The Way that you Breathe

You may be asking what this has to do with meditation, but it has everything to do with it. When you breathe incorrectly, you may just be allowing too much oxygen into your system. People who panic do this as well as people who get overly excited about things. They breathe more air and sometimes the excitement makes other parts of the body respond. For example, when you have too much oxygen in the system, your blood pressure may rise, or you may find that you cannot sit calmly but are too excited. In the Western world, people are subjected to input all of the time. That means that you have noise in your life. TV, crowds, cell phones, work routines, rushing around, worrying about kids are all things that get in the way of slowing up your mind. There is at the current time an epidemic of stress-related illnesses. Although these things happen in countries that are more accustomed to meditation, you have to remember that meditation came first and that these people are accustomed to the process of meditation. In the Western world, people are not.

Try an exercise to help you to understand about breathing because this will help you when you start to meditate.

Breathe in and count to eight. Then breathe out and count to ten. Many Westerners breathe through the mouth and this isn't the best way to breathe since quite often, you swallow air which causes wind or other digestive problems. You need to use your nostrils and while you are breathing in this manner, sit with your back straight. There is a reason for this. Throughout the spinal area, you have something very important to your wellbeing – these are energy points that are otherwise known as chakra. If you try breathing in a slouched position, you may just be blocking these chakras which is why it's important to learn how vital posture is while you breathe.

Try to carry on breathing in this manner with your eyes closed and put all thoughts out of your mind. You may have heard the expression:

"If you want to conquer the anxiety of life, live in the moment, live in the breath." – Amit Ray

What he means by this is that you should be totally conscious of your breathing and be there, feeling the air or energy going into your body and being conscious of it as it leaves your body, putting all other thoughts out of your mind. If you try this, it will probably not be long before you start to find things to think about. We have compartments in the brain and people who are not yet disciplined enough to meditate don't realize how often they open the lids of these compartments or what they contain. For example, if you think about the past or worry about the future, you are not being in the breath at all. You are escaping into the past or the future rather than being in the moment and that's what meditation is all about.

However, you should never be upset that thoughts come. It is your job to control these thoughts and not allow them to control you. Carry on breathing in this manner and if you place your hand upon your upper abdomen, you should feel it increase in size when you inhale and decrease when you exhale. Think of that rather than anything else and try to keep the rhythm of your breathing the same so that there is a steady flow in and out of your body. This deep kind of breathing helps you during meditation and should be the thing that you concentrate on while meditating, but don't think too deeply about it. You should merely be aware of what is happening as you breathe, without actually focusing. Let me try and explain.

There are times in life when you do things without thinking. As you go through your meditation practice every day, this will also become a habit that you do without really thinking about it and that's the best way to go. If you attach to much importance to your failure or success, you are not in the breath and that's the whole point of meditation. However, if you are worried about what you are doing, it's hard to be there either. Thus, just breathe. After a while, you will feel the rhythm of your breathing and won't have to count anymore because it just happens. When you achieve that, you are ready to meditate and to be in the breath.

As the last moment of thought on the subject of being in the now, it may help you to read something that was written by the Dalai Lama when he was asked what surprised him most about mankind. His answer is very astute.

"Man... Because he sacrifices his health in order to make money. Then he sacrifices money to recuperate his health. And then he is so anxious about the future that he does not enjoy the present; the result being that he does not live in the present or the future; he lives as if he is never going to die, and then dies having never really lived." – The Dalai Lama

It helps you to make sense of being mindful when you are breathing. What he says in effect is that we are living our lives without being aware of the moment and that all of these moments are passing and our lives are not actually being lived. It may help you with your breathing to read this quotation before you start the exercise. Sit in a position that is comfortable on a hard dining chair and it's a good idea to place your feet flat on the floor. If you have clothing that is at all restrictive, change into something that allows you to relax and feel comfortable.

Then try and breathe in the way we suggested above, counting to 8 on the inhale and 10 on the exhale. Do it over and over again. While you do this, you will find that your blood pressure reduces and your heartbeat goes down and that's something that you should expect when you meditate. It's perfectly normal and it's a good idea to have a notebook next to you so that before you go rushing back into your busy life, you make notes of your meditation session, and write down things that you think you may be able to do better next time. Perhaps there is a draft from a window. Perhaps something distracted you. Note these things because they will help you to avoid the same distractions the next time that you meditate.

Take it easy and take it at a pace that is comfortable for you. Sit and breathe. Think of nothing except the breath. Practice at this and you will find that your meditation is more effective, because you know what to expect. Think of the quotation of the Dalai Lama and tell yourself that you are happy to be in the moment, rather than allowing your thoughts to drag you into the past or into worries for a future that has not happened yet and may never happen. All that you can be sure of is that the now exists. It is transient and ever changing. Thus, grab it while it is here and enjoy the exercise suggested.

Chapter Three: Emptying the Mind

Since you are accustomed to thinking a multitude of thoughts during the course of your day, it is also a good idea to learn to let go of thoughts. Negative thoughts have a negative impact on our lives. When you hold onto anger, the person who suffers the most is not that person who made you angry, but you yourself. Chances are that this person isn't even thinking about the event that upset you. Thus, you empower others to control the way that your emotions hit you if you persist in playing around with negative thoughts of any kind. Jealousy and hate come into this range of negative thoughts and it's far better to think positive things when you are not meditating because it helps you to become a positive person and have a positive influence on the people you care about. However, how do you get rid of thoughts when they come involuntarily? That's the problem that many people who meditate have when they are new to the practice. Some people use chanting meditation to help to clear those thoughts, while others learn to let go and that's what this chapter is all about.

What thoughts do you have in the course of a normal day that you are able to let go of without even thinking about it?

Well, although you may not be aware of it, there are thousands of thoughts that happen during the course of 24 hours that you give no importance to. When you are driving the car, how much thought do you give to someone who crosses the road at the traffic lights right in front of your stopped car? How much thought do you give the driver in the car next to you? We are surrounded by things that are fleeting. As I already explained, each moment of your life offers different triggers that lead to thoughts and these thoughts may be:

- Negative
- Positive
- Neutral

Since you give very little importance to neutral thoughts, it sounds very much as if you need to neutralize the thoughts that you have that fall into the other two categories when you want to meditate. What that means is letting them go. So how can you do that? Negative thoughts don't enhance your life. They make you think of bad things and your mind may waste much time thinking about past hurts or things that people have said to you. These thoughts serve very little purpose. To let them go, think of the thoughts as being a little like objects in the street that you pass while you are driving and simply cut them off. Imagine them to have no more importance than those things which you naturally cut off anyway. If you want to make it an amusing exercise, think of them as pieces of paper floating down in the sky and disappearing from sight.

The most important thing in all of this is to switch off a natural instinct, which is to judge. When you see something, you tend to jump to conclusions and judge it. Judgment will get in the way of being able to let go. For example, if you think of an ex-boyfriend or ex-girlfriend, it's very hard to step away from judgment because you think you know what the situation was and how unreasonable those circumstances were. However, they are passed. They form no part of who you are today unless you empower them by judging the thoughts. Let go. When you do, this is the best empowerment that you can possibly achieve because all the time you let thoughts persuade you in one direction or another, you empower those thoughts and they become almost impossible to let go of. Being able to do this will empower you in your life in general but will certainly aid you when it comes to meditation because you will see those thoughts for what they are. They are invasions and by letting go, you begin to free your mind ready for that step into meditation.

Try it during the course of your day when people say things to you. Try dropping judgment and enabling yourself because when you do that, you tend to be more empathetic and don't say things in haste that you may regret at a later time. Distancing yourself from your thoughts will become easier if you are able to learn to let go. This is also a great exercise to use to let go of negativity and start to feel good about life.

Chapter Four: Mindfulness

You probably have memories of childhood and may well have been told to watch your manners and be mindful of how you behave. Mindfulness extends a little further than that and many adults don't feel mindful as they go through their everyday chores or things that they have to do. Basically, this means being in the moment that you are living in. The best way to describe mindfulness is being aware of all of your senses. If you take a walk in the garden in the early morning, you will be able to use mindfulness to really enjoy the experience. Wrap up warm, and take a stroll and you will probably see many things you have never seen before because you haven't really looked. What about the cobwebs that have been spun overnight? Did you see them and the dew drops that hang from them and look like jewels? Did you notice that?

Mindfulness means using every sense that you have and if you incorporate this into your life, you are embracing all the opportunities that come your way and making the most of them and that's very important to people who meditate. To be present in the breath is something that doesn't come naturally to people whose worlds are filled with chaos. Thus, sometimes you need to step back and use the senses that you were given when you were born and feel the earth around you, hear the noises of nature, touch the textures and taste the flavors of life. Being mindful really do go hand in hand with meditational practice. It means stilling yourself at this very moment. Whether you are simply observing the world or drinking a cup of coffee, mindfulness makes that small experience into a real experience. You may be wondering what I mean by that, but how often have you eaten your sandwiches without really noticing the taste of what you are eating? The trouble with this world of overload is that we are encouraged by our peers and by advertisements to get things done and do them quickly and thus, we lose the ability to use our senses in the way that they were intended to be used.

When you are mindful, you are completely absorbed in the moment. You may be cleaning floors, but if you are, your attention will be on every detail of cleaning that floor. Although this may seem a very banal task, it's every bit as important as everything else that you do if you do it intentionally and pays attention to each detail, instead of allowing yourself to be constantly interrupted and finding no joy in the job at all.

Mindful eating is something you can begin to practice. Forget about what happened this morning or what may happen this afternoon. Simply sit down to your food and enjoy every mouthful, chewing it correctly and distinguishing between taste and textures. Not only will you be doing your digestive system a favor but you will also start to enjoy your food and drink instead of simply thinking of it as fuel that goes in one end and comes out the other. Try a variety of fruit. Try different salad vegetables and really enjoy them. It isn't about speed anymore. It's about being in the moment.

Similarly, if you choose to listen to a piece of music, make that your focus. Turn off all other intrusions into your life and let the music absorb your interest. Listen to each note and every nuance because when you do, you enjoy the music more and can stay in the moment without letting thoughts get in the way of your enjoyment. You may not see the connection to meditation yet, but you will with time. What happens when you are capable of switching off the entire disturbance of life is allow yourself to be in the moment and be in the breath and that's what meditation is all about. Many cannot stand the silence. Many need more than that, but if you are going to drown out the silence with music, then make sure it's music that allows you to be there in the moment rather than just using it as background noise.

When you learn to be mindful, you are also cautious with your replies and your judgments and we have already told you what judgments are worth. They don’t help you to let go of thoughts and they often put words into your mouth that you regret at a later date. Thus, if you find yourself presented with any kind of situation that makes you feel negative, breathe and let your thoughts see things from a clearer perspective, without the added element of judgment. Be mindful in your replies and you will find that you will be able to slow down and keep your mind in check, rather than succumbing to the negativity others wish on you.

Chapter Five: Preparing for Meditation

As you intend to incorporate meditation into your life, it may help you to know a little more about why it's a good thing and what you will need in order to meditate. As far as tools go, you really don't actually need anything, but if you want to commit yourself to the process of meditation, it helps to give yourself the incentive to make this a daily part of your life if you create an area where you will meditate. This shows some form of commitment if you prepare the space with a yoga mat, a meditation stool or hard cushion and decorate the area in a very inspirational way.

When you look in Buddhist temples, one of the first things that you notice is the altar. It is decorated in pastel colors and floral designs for a purpose. This purpose is to inspire. Thus, in your home space for meditation, it helps to have objects that inspire you and each person will see their own needs for inspiration in different ways. For example, you may want a Buddha statue because you find this pleasing and aesthetic. You may want candles as candles can be used for certain types of meditation. You may want inspirational pictures or even a Tibetan singing bowl. This is very useful if you are going to chant with your meditation, but even if you are not, the sound of this instrument can be used to get you into the right frame of mind for meditation. As I said before, Buddhism isn't a religion. People don't worship Buddha. They use him as inspiration. It isn't an altar in the traditional sense but is an altar to inspire those who choose to visit the temple.

The things to look out for in the area that you choose are the following:

- Potential distractions from a window
- Drafts that come into the room from doorways
- The silence factor – is the room peaceful?
- The comfort factor – Is the temperature comfortable?
- The seating – Will you be comfortable for the duration of your meditation?
- Your clothing – Is this something non-restrictive?

When you are happy with all of this, you then need to be able to relax in that area you have chosen. What about some inspirational works? I think that reading Buddhist philosophy that isn't too heavy will give you the push to keep up your meditation practice and there are some splendid books on quotations that you can use although of course, these are not necessary. They just help your mind prepare for the positivity that meditation will give you. Some suggested reading would be Quotations by Rumi, The Prophet by Khalil Gibran and anything that is written by the Dalai Lama because all of these books help to educate you in philosophy and get you into the right frame of mind to follow through and that's important at this stage. Many people try meditation and give up because their expectations are different from the reality or because they feel that they are not succeeding at meditation, which is a nonsense because meditation is basically so simple. The attitude that you approach meditation with will help you to want to keep it up and you may even find that you are prepared to give meditation more time than the twenty minutes suggested once you start to realize the benefits of the practice.

The ambient light in the room where you meditate can also make a difference. If you are in light that is too harsh, this can even penetrate your mind when you have your eyes closed, so try to choose an area that is reasonably lit, but not startlingly so.

Lastly, do inform people that you live with that you are not to be disturbed during your meditation. You may even find that others in your entourage are happy to try meditation too. The most important thing is that they respect your choice and you can also use the reason that you want to improve your life and feel better about it and that work is causing you too much stress in your life. As stress is well-known these days, this may be enough for your family to respect that you need silent time for twenty minutes a day while you do your meditation. You may even want to hang a “do not disturb” sign on your door to remind those that you live with that this is not a good time for you to be disturbed by others.

Chapter Six: Concentration Meditation

In concentration meditation, you focus on one thing at a time and that thing can be your breath, an image of something that soothes you, a peaceful sound or even an object like the flame of a candle. That's one of the reasons that I suggested that you have candles in your meditation space. How does this help? Well, focusing on just one thing increases your ability to focus and decreases your tendency to get distracted by things or situations. There is a particular way to concentrate that you need to try and get accustomed to. It's not like when you concentrate on learning or on a particular book. You are not trying to input information. Instead, it could be described as a stare or concentration on not being pulled into thinking or looking at anything else.

Since anxiety or stress often arise from unnecessary distractions like thoughts of the past or worries of the future, which hold no value in your present, when you practice concentration meditation and master the skill of focusing on one thing at a time, you combat stress by only focusing on the actions you need to take to get rid of the stress. Believe it or not, when you do this kind of meditation, you let go of worldly thoughts and that helps because it gives your subconscious mind a rest from all of the stimulation that it is accustomed to.

So how exactly should you practice concentration meditation to fight stress and anxiety ultimately? We will discuss that next:

How to Practice Concentration Meditation

Here are the steps on how to perform concentration meditation:

- **Choose a Calm Place:** First, find a quiet place to meditate where nobody can disturb you while you meditate; it can be your room or a spot under the tree in your backyard. Make sure to keep all distractions away from you; switch off your phone when you sit in the meditation spot and switch off any noisy appliances. If you can get away from the ringing of the telephone and the noise of the world, in general, this will help you to be able to meditate successfully.

- **Relax:** Once you are at your chosen place to meditate, get comfortable; you can sit cross legged, sit on the sofa or lay down on the couch - whatever pose makes you feel relaxed. The important thing is that you make sure that your back is straight, no matter which position you use. For people who are new to meditation, I would suggest that if you sit on the ground under a tree, you bend your knees and cross your ankles.

Tip 1: If you are sitting indoors, dim the lights and light some candles. Why do you need to do that? Well, lighting candles create a soothing environment thus allowing you to meditate easily. But if lighting candles isn't your thing, then hang an image of something that soothes you on the wall you are going to be facing while meditating. It is a good idea to have subdued lighting so that you are not distracted from what you are doing easily.

Tip 2: Set a timer: The purpose of meditation is to increase your focus, which you can lose if you get distracted by seeing the clock every minute. Set up a timer, so you don't have to worry about checking the time on your watch again and again. Make sure to keep your meditation sessions short in the beginning and gradually increase them as you progress. The timer should be one that does not tick as the tick, tick of a timer can distract you.

5-10 minute sessions work best at the start and you can have these sessions twice a day. Once you get used to it, increase the time of sessions to get better results. I always suggest to beginners that they use 15 minutes as the time to put aside for meditation as that gives you enough time to set yourself up and also to write in your journal after you have finished meditating while your heartbeat and blood pressure get back to normal.

- **Focus on One Thing:** Once you are through to the aforementioned steps, take a deep breath and focus on one thing. For the purpose of this example, I am considering that you are focusing on an image you placed in front of you, the flame of the candle you lit or just your breath - it's entirely up to you.

  Start noticing the detailing of the image. For instance, if it's an image of a cow grazing in the field, then focus on each detail of the image like what is the color of the cow? Or how many spots does that cow have? etc. If you have decided to use a candle, then concentrate on the flicker of the candle and relax into your concentration so that you are breathing deeply and not really taking notice of anything except the flame of the candle. If you decide to concentrate on your breath, then breathe into the count of 8 and breathe out to the count of ten and keep the rhythm of your breathing constant. You are not accustomed to breathing this deeply and this is what puts you in a relaxing state.

Tip: Set Aside Thoughts That Distract You: When you try to focus on just one thing, in this case, an image, your mind will try every possible way to distract you (it just has a way of running on autopilot!). It will bring in thoughts of the past or something that relates to your current situation or something that you forgot to do.

If that happens, then bring your attention back to the picture you are seeing. Repeat this action of bringing your focus back to the picture until your alarm goes off. It may seem impossible at the start to focus on only one thing, but you have to be patient and persistent at the same time.

You need to appreciate that this form of meditation requires a lot of your attention and if you fail, you should not get angry about it or even frustrated since this is bound to happen. Just go back to thinking about the breath and feel the breath going into your body and then leaving your body. Think in terms of energy and try to give a visual to the movement of air as this helps you to concentrate on it.

Keep practicing concentration meditation until you completely start focusing on one thing at a time throughout the 5-10 minute sessions. Once you feel that your mind doesn't get distracted throughout the session, you will notice a great reduction in your stress levels. Even then, you can continue meditation to increase your focus more and more, which will only increase your ability to combat stress.

Now that you have learnt how to let go of distracting thoughts and focus on one thing at a time to relax, we will learn how to work on the stress triggering thoughts and calm them for good in the next chapter. While we have already talked about letting go, it is something that is so important that the chapters in this book have been written to try and get you to concentrate on that aspect more than anything else. After a while, you will find that you want more time to meditate and that's okay too. Just take your time and enjoy what you are doing. The best times of day are first thing in the morning and before your evening meal. That way, you are not distracted by the noises your tummy makes after eating or struggling with the digestive process during your meditation session.

Chapter Seven: Mindfulness Meditation

One of the major reasons you become anxious is because you think of the horrible past experiences all the time or you try to analyze the future, which is always uncertain.

The problem with both thinking patterns is that you get lost in something that has either already happened or yet to come making you forgetful of the sensitivity of the situation you are currently in. This not only increases your workload but also increases your stress levels making you anxious. Thus, this type of meditation is useful for people who have problems quieting the mind.

Mindfulness meditation is a great technique to train yourself to live in the moment and keep focusing on the present moment as it passes. It is a great technique to remove stress and anxiety as it (mindfulness) grounds you in the present. Many classes that you take in yoga teach you all about grounding and the position that you take during your meditation will also help you with this aspect of meditation.

By practicing mindfulness meditation, you can get rid of this problem (the autopilot mode whereby you are either thinking of the future or the past) by only focusing on the present moment. Not only do you disregard the unnecessary worries of past or future, but you also start to enjoy your present more. As a result, your stress levels decrease and you live a peaceful and happy life. It basically does that by making you more aware of your thoughts, emotions and feelings.

How Mindfulness Meditation Helps You

This type of meditation allows you to explore your thoughts and sensations and understand their essence. Instead of shunning negative thoughts or labeling them as good or bad, you try to comprehend them better and figure out why you feel a certain way. This allows you to get to the root cause of things and eliminate those causes, which automatically helps you make peace with troubling thoughts.

If you feel you're a failure, you try to explore why you feel that way. You learn to acknowledge this thought and the stress that comes with it and accept it as an emotion instead of abandoning it altogether. When you accept it, you don't become bothered by it anymore and try to settle it peacefully and non-judgmentally. This helps you stay focused on how you can improve your present and makes you stop worrying about your past or future. Remember at this point what the Dalai Lama said about mankind because it is very relevant.

Moreover, this practice makes you more patient and gentle with yourself and allows you to accept yourself completely. When self-acceptance occurs, you become more open to who you are and fully embrace yourself. This automatically reduces the stress associated with not accepting your individuality. This is particularly useful for people who may be suffering from self-esteem issues. All of those thoughts do not amount to who you are. You need to understand the root of those thoughts and then accept that you are who you are and not judge it by what other people say.

Training yourself to be mindful at all times is hard to achieve, but once you achieve it, your ability to fight stress, anxiety and depression effortlessly will have improved greatly.

So how exactly can you be mindful in your everyday life? Let's learn how to go about it:

How to Practice Mindfulness Meditation

The first 3 steps of practicing mindfulness meditation are the same as the ones you practiced in concentration meditation.

These steps are: choose a calm place, relax and set a timer. You also need to be seated in a position that respects your spine. Thus, if you are on a hard chair, sit up straight so that energy can pass down to your energy points. Place your feet flat on the floor. If you want to feel even more grounded, kick your shoes off and feel your naked feet on the floor.

Since I have mentioned each step in detail in the previous chapter, I am not repeating them again. Here are the additional steps you need to perform to become mindful at all times.

It is also a good idea to write down what you want to gain from your meditation and writing in your journal before you start meditation will help to guide your meditation and help you to solve problems that relate to your self-esteem or the problems that present themselves in your life.

- **Settle Your Mind:** Once you sit comfortably feeling relaxed, detach your mind from all the thoughts of the things going on in your life. It might take a while for you to completely forget everything going around especially if you had a stressful day.

  If such is the case, you will notice that your mind is dancing from one thought to another. Don't force it to calm down; just let the thoughts be. Let it dance for a while and once it settles down, bring your focus to meditation, which at the start may feel a strange concept to you but its okay if you feel this way. Again, if you filled out your thoughts in your meditation book, don't let them go further by continuing to think of them. Just acknowledge that they are there but give them no more credence than that. They are just thoughts.

- **Use Your Breath to Become Focused:** Once your mind is settled down and your focus is totally on meditation, bring your awareness to your breath as you take it.

  Focus on the inhalations and exhalations of each breath. Feel how the air enters your nostrils and then flows through your windpipe into your lungs and then comes back from your lungs to your windpipe then nose and then gets out of your body. Remember the counting that you did when you did the breathing exercises in this book? These will help you because you need to develop a deep breathing rhythm that is steady and if you need to use counting at the beginning, of course, you can do this until you feel comfortable that the amount of breath is just right.

Your mind may come up with a thought to distract you. If that happens, ignore it and bring back your focus to your breath. Keep in mind that focusing on the actions you are doing right now is itself a practice to become mindful.

Whenever a thought pops up in your mind, instead of fighting with it, just let it flow. Bring in this alternate thought, "Oh! I need to focus on my breath" and then replace it with the action of focusing on your breath. The thing that you need to learn is to acknowledge a thought rather than pretending it isn't there, and simply tell it to go away because you are busy at this time. When you do that, don't attach any emotions to the thought and view it just like it's a scene that is passing you while you are sitting on a train. Judgment is human failure and when you are able to let go of this in your life, you will find that it's much easier to meditate.

- **Explore One Thought At A Time:** Once you feel more focused and calm, let yourself a little loose and don't shun away any thought that enters your mind. Now your job is to explore them and know yourself better. If you feel any sensation, emotion or feeling, hold on to it and try to understand it better. Ask yourself questions like 'Why do I feel that way?', 'What exactly happened that made me feel this way?' and similar questions. By asking such questions, you try to identify the reason behind that emotion and thought. Make sure not to label any emotion or thought as good or bad, negative or positive; accept it wholeheartedly. Be very patient with it and use it to know yourself better. After doing it for a few minutes, you'll find something new about yourself and the way you think. For instance, you may discover that you feel you're a failure because you don't work hard and this makes you realize the importance of working hard on your goal. This makes you realize your problem and gives you a fix for it too. When your mind is quiet and thoughts arrive, you can explore them and do this very logically instead of involving your emotions and judgment which is when thoughts go haywire.

Repeat this exercise of mindfulness meditation twice a day for 5-10 minutes per session at the start and increase the timing of each session as you progress. Explore new thoughts daily and understand them better to get a true insight into your mind.

As you do that, try to bring mindfulness meditation into each and every aspect of your life as well. What does that mean? Why am I feeling this way? You are perfectly entitled to acknowledge thoughts but not to let them take over your mind to the extent that they impose emotions upon you. When you find that you have had enough of thoughts, go back to being in the moment, in the breath and concentrate on the breath instead of thinking, shunning the thoughts that you really do not wish to deal with at this time or which you know will make you emotional. You are in control of this moment. You can go back to concentrating on the breath at any time. Just think to yourself that this kind of meditation helps to make you aware of your thoughts and the reasons that they occur. However, try to carry on this line of thinking even after you have meditated, because it helps you to accept thoughts, to process them without emotions and to move on to the next thought in your everyday life.

You will see from the next section that you can bring mindfulness meditation into everyday actions and this helps you as a continuance of your mindfulness meditation sessions to accept life as it is, rather than wishing it was different. We cannot change who we are. All that we can change is our approach to life and mindfulness brings you back into the moment, so you don't miss anything along the way.

Bringing Mindfulness Meditation into Every Aspect of Your Life

This means that you have to be fully involved in everything you do without thinking of anything else or jumping to another task. If you are reading a book, focus on it completely and don't let your mind wander off in thought to something else. Tell yourself 'I have to focus on the book right now' and try to enjoy each word of it. The more you focus on it, the more you become involved in it. This helps you stay in the present and live each moment of it fully.

Similarly, if you are doing laundry, be fully involved in it, so you do or think of nothing else but the act you're involved in right now. It will take you a little time to be mindful of each moment all the time, but practice will help you get there for sure; and when that happens, you'll unlock a beautiful, happy life that will keep you stress-free at all times.

We were never intended to multi task. It really goes against the natural workings of the brain and when you learn to concentrate totally on everything that you do, it takes a whole load of strain off the mind. You also get more done and can work out your goals and really make an effort to reach them, one step at a time. You can make all kinds of tasks meaningful by paying attention to what it is you are doing. I remember one day cleaning the tiles in the shower and thinking how much they sparkle and shine when in the past I would never really have noticed the fruits of my own labor. It was a moment that I enjoyed as I could see my smiling face in the reflection and had used mindfulness to get me through everything that I had to do before folks dropped in to stay at my house.

While you work on this, do introduce body scan meditation into your routine too. It is an excellent technique to get rid of the stress stuck in your body and become fully relaxed. The next chapter talks about it.

Chapter Eight: Body Scan Meditation

Body scan meditation helps reduce stress by making you aware of how your body feels instead of paying attention to stressful thoughts. When you feel stressed out, your body also feels those effects and it starts to show signs of stress through pain in your back, stomach or tensed shoulders. You may even experience neck ache, particularly if you have been concentrating on things that were difficult and that strained you in some way. You may just have aching bones because you are cold or because you feel worn out in general, but a body scan can help you to feel much better.

By practicing body scan meditation, you distract your mind from the stressful thoughts by paying attention to those parts of the body that feel stressed. As a result, you become mindful of your body and forgetful of the thoughts that bring you stress. Thus, you feel relaxed and your stress levels greatly reduce.

Here is a step-by-step guide on how you can perform this meditation technique.

How to Perform Body Scan Meditation

The first step is to find a quiet place to perform this meditation technique, which is similar to the other techniques that I have mentioned earlier. Once you are in a quiet place with no distractions, then follow the steps mentioned below:

- Lie on your back on the floor in a position that makes you feel comfortable. Make sure that your posture doesn't make you uncomfortable. If lying on the floor hurts, then you can lie on a mattress or bed instead; there is no hard and fast rule that you have to lie on the floor.

  The aim here for you is to feel comfortable. You can slide a pillow under your back if you feel uneasy or you can lie on your side: right or left- whichever makes you feel relaxed. The preferred position is on your back using only one pillow to support your head so that your airways are clear.

- As soon as you settle, take a deep breath to calm your racing mind. Sometimes, it may take you longer than just one deep breath depending on how your day went. If that's the case, keep breathing deeply until you feel a sense of calmness in your mind. A great way to calm your racing mind is to focus on the breath as you take it. In fact, if it helps you, use the counting that you used before – 8 for the intake of breath through the nostrils and 10 for the exhale. You can even see if you are breathing deeply enough by placing a hand on your upper abdomen and feeling it going up when you breathe in and down when you exhale.

- Once your mind is calm, bring your attention to your body. Feel every sensation in it. Start with the tingling feeling in your toes and feet. Once you feel it, slowly shift your attention from your feet to other parts of your body. Feel the tension in each part as you move up from your toes to your head.

  Feel the tension in the muscles of your legs and the sensations in your belly or the tension in your shoulders and back depending on where you feel the most stress and pain. Feel the strain in your head and your eyelids hurt as you open and close them.
  Note: In the process of examining every sensation in your body, your mind will try to distract you by bringing in different thoughts. If that happens, bring your focus back to your body and start again from the

toes and slowly move up to the head and try again to feel the tension on each part. If it helps you at all, I find that being conscious of that area of the body, followed by tensing the area and then purposely relaxing it helps a lot. As you relax that part of the body, feel the weight as the body relaxes.

- Do this exercise for 15-20 minutes at the start and then slowly increase the time, as you get good at it. Remember that your mind is your #1 enemy, as it keeps distracting you from bringing in countless thoughts that only end up causing stress and anxiety. However, you have to fight it (which is a continuous struggle); with time and patience, everything can be achieved.

- Body scan meditation is hard as compared to the other techniques that I have mentioned before but, if done properly, it is a great technique, as it can greatly help you to relieve stress and anxiety almost instantly. It also helps to lower your blood pressure and bring your heartbeat down, so do remember to get up slowly from the exercise and relax for a moment before going into your everyday activities again.

So far, you have learnt three of the most effective meditation techniques to reduce stress and anxiety. To get better results, it is important to enhance their effectiveness. The next chapter discusses some great tips and tricks to enhance the effectiveness of these meditative practices.

Chapter Nine: Tips and Tricks to Improve the Effectiveness of Meditation

Meditation helps you relieve stress regardless of the technique you use to practice it. However, there are some tips and tricks that you can apply to enhance the results and increase its effectiveness. Follow the tips mentioned below to get enhanced results.

1: Meditate Twice a Day

If you want to see great results in a short period, then you need to make meditation a regular practice. The best time to meditate is at sunrise and sunset or 6am and 6pm. At these times, there are hardly any distractions and interruptions around you, which allows you to meditate easily and effectively.

In addition, you need to at least meditate twice a day. The effects of one small session of less than 30 minutes don't last for more than 12 hours. Therefore, to feel peaceful and relaxed at all times, it is best to meditate at least twice daily. If you meditate for around an hour and have quite a hectic routine, it's alright to meditate once a day too. However, make sure to stick to this practice and make it a routine. You can also use meditation during your working day in the manner I have suggested helping to calm you and to help you to concentrate on things that are important to you. Meditation awakens the mind and that can be very useful to you in your lunch break, but be sure to do it before you eat rather than trying to do so afterwards.

Secondly, always meditate at the exact same time. If you meditate at 5pm on the first two days, ensure to meditate at the exact time daily. This practice cultivates consistency and punctuality making you regular with meditation. What you may not realize is that habits are formed by repetition. This is true of any habit and adding the habit of meditation to another daily habit will help. This form of habit stacking has been proven to be very effective. What this means is listing things that you do every day at set times. For example, you get up at a set time – so you can meditate on it. You get home from work at a set time and probably sit down and have a coffee or a tea. You can choose this moment to meditate. The point is that with repetition each day of the habit of meditation it will become second nature and part of your daily routine.

In fact, with practice, you will easily get into meditation without trying too much since your body will know 'it is time to meditate' when that time comes. You should also turn off all distractions during your meditation time so that you can concentrate on just being instead of worrying about whether the phone will go off or someone will knock at the door. By choosing a meditation time, you also get those who live with you accustomed to respecting this time that you put to one side for meditation.

2: Eat something but don't be too full

Try to meditate on an empty stomach to easily focus on the practice. When you have just had a meal, your stomach is full, which often makes you lethargic. If you meditate at this time, you're likely to lose focus on the practice and drift off to sleep instead. You may also find that your digestive system makes it too difficult to sit still in the same position and concentrate on just being. Your stomach may be making noises and uncomfortable in an upright position.

However, if you feel really hungry at the time of your meditation session, then eat something light such as a fruit or a piece of chocolate so you can stay alert and concentrate on your meditation and don't become distracted during the practice due to an empty stomach. I always take a glass of water into the room with me as well as this may help to stave off any hunger or stop you from craving food during your practice.

3: Meditate at the Same Place

Try to dedicate one place to your meditation spot and don't do anything else there. By practicing meditation at the same spot every day and not doing anything else on that spot, you will naturally feel like meditating whenever you go to that spot. As a result, it will be a lot easier to build a habit of meditating when you have a dedicated spot that makes it very easy for you to get into meditation. As we have already mentioned, having a space set aside for meditation will make you more serious about the practice because you will have devoted the space to something you are trying to incorporate into your life and it will be wasted if you do not use it for that purpose. You may have to make adjustments if you find that you are getting sidetracked by noise or by too much light. You will find that perfect spot and when you do, will see the sense in having one particular place in which to meditate. It helps to reinforce the habit.

4: Minimize Interruptions

Put on a "do-not-disturb" sign on the door of your room before you start meditating. Also, switch off your cell phone to remain focused; if you can't do that, just put it on the silent mode so there is nothing that holds you back and you can completely focus on your practice. Minimizing interruptions will increase your concentration in your practice resulting in better performance. Let people know that this is a time when you need to be alone and need silence. Most people who are aware that you are doing this for your health will respect that you need to be alone. You can also put your phone on answering machine and place a sign on the door of your house to not disturb you for the next twenty minutes or so.

5: Write your Thoughts before Practicing Meditation

One thing that you are likely to struggle with as a beginner is experiencing distracting thoughts while meditating. You can escape this problem with a simple solution. Before starting the session, write down all the thoughts that cross your mind. By doing this, you tell yourself that you have this thought on record, which you will deal with later when the time is right.

For instance, if you wrote everything that came to your mind including the thought of ironing your clothes as you won't get the time tomorrow as you have to leave for office early, it will be easy for you to focus. In fact, if this thought disturbs you, you can relax your mind by telling yourself that you have it on your notice and you will do it when the time is right. This comforts you and helps you return your attention to meditation.

Follow this writing of thoughts with an additional note of why you are meditating, to try and reinforce the idea. You can also add thoughts of things that you are grateful for before you meditate as this puts you in a positive state of mind.

Moreover, also create your meditation journal. Write down your feelings in it before and after meditating every day to understand how you felt after each session. A meditation journal also helps you to understand your weaknesses, which you can work for the next time. Do go through this journal once every week to track your performance and feel good about yourself. If you feel you're doing a great job, treat yourself to something nice to encourage yourself to meditate regularly and develop a habit of it.

Many people write an introductory prayer for their meditation which reminds them of the purpose of meditation and betterment of their approach. This is useful if you are finding it hard to find the incentive to concentrate over a period of time and feel that your efforts are not paying off. You may not feel the benefits straight away. It takes time and persistence, but once you make this a habit, it is certain that you will enjoy your meditation sessions and use them as a better way to get to know who you are and what you want out of life.

6: Use Mudras to get Enhanced Results

Mudras are hand or body positions that influence your energy, mood and feelings. Mostly, the fingers and hands are held in some position, but your entire body can be used to form a mudra too. Here we will discuss some hand mudras to relieve stress and become happy, as it is believed your fingers have nerve connections that connect to different parts of your brain to produce different emotions. Here are some amazing mudras to let go of stress and become happy and peaceful.

1. Tse Mudra to relieve stress

Tse Mudra is well known and is considered as one of the best mudras to combat anxiety and depression. According to Chinese tradition, this mudra is practiced to drive away stress, sadness, fear and brings good luck. It is said that this mudra also increases your intuitive ability. Given below are images followed by the instructions on how to practice this mudra in your meditation.

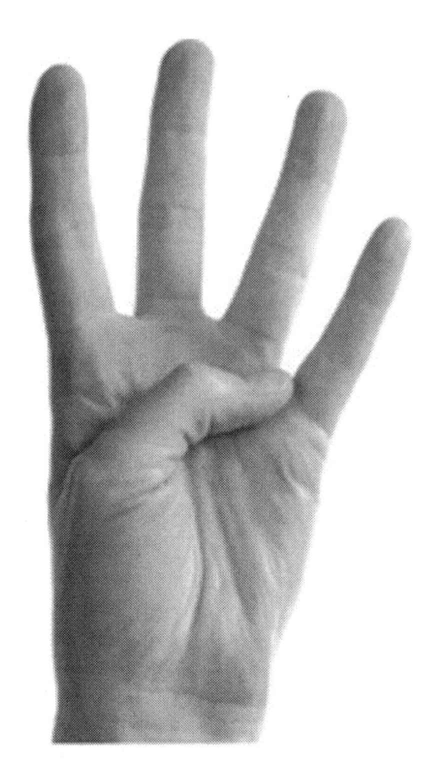

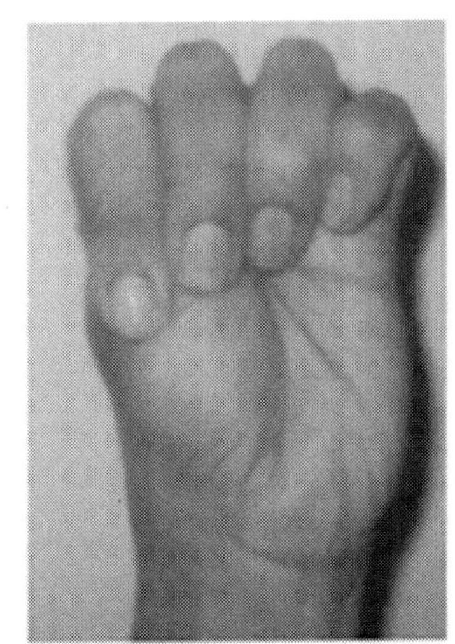

- When you're sitting or lying in your comfortable position for meditation, place your thumbs on your thighs.

- Now put your thumb between your little and ring finger as you can see in the first picture. Do this with both hands.

- Now encircle your thumb with your other four fingers as you can see it in the second picture.

- Hold this position in your hands throughout your meditation session.

When you incorporate this mudra, you will notice that your stress levels drop more than when you meditate without this mudra.

2.Ksepana Mudra

It is also a very helpful mudra to improve the effectiveness of meditation as well as to increase your inner peace and happiness. This mudra is known for its magical powers to release all the negativity that is being ingested within your soul. You can use this mudra in your meditation especially in those cases where you had a very bad day and you are flooding with negative emotions. Given below is an image that shows the Ksepana mudra along with instructions on how to incorporate this mudra into your meditation.

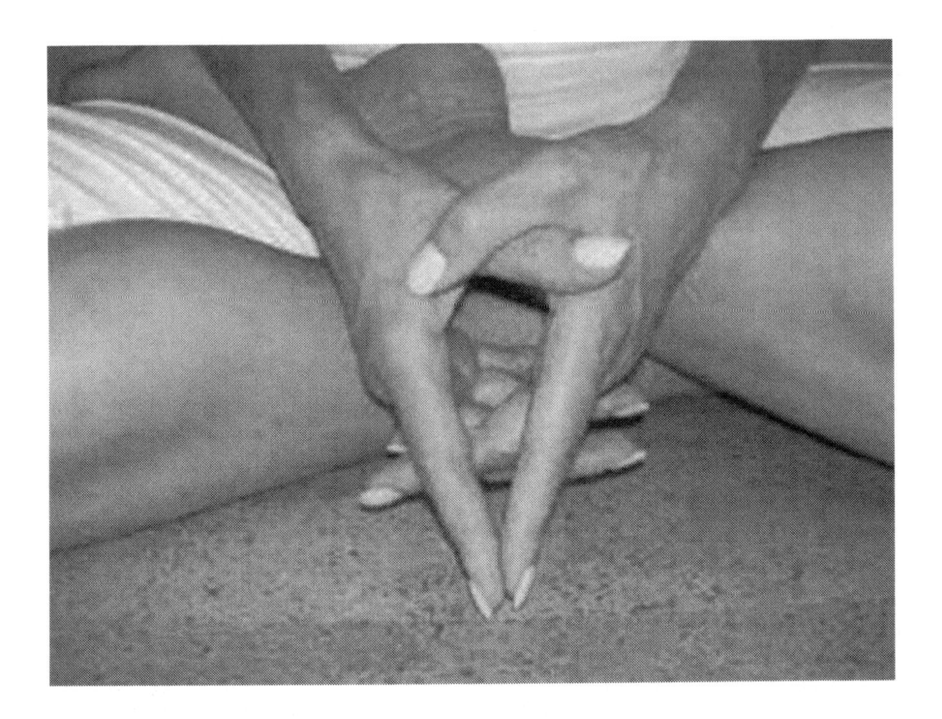

- When you start your session and get a comfortable posture, clasp both hands: all the fingers crossing each other.

- Then take out both index fingers and join their tips as you can see in the picture above.

- Now drop your hands pointing to the ground. Hold this position for at least 2 minutes, or you can hold it to the entire length of the session.

You will notice great effects after your session ends as the negative thoughts that were flowing through your mind before the session will have greatly reduced.

3. Prana Mudra

Practicing Prana mudra is a good way to collect energy from the universe. Therefore, you can use this mudra to get energized, brighten up your mood and reduce your stress levels. Use this mudra on days when you feel drained out and you don't feel like doing anything because of the energy deficiency. See the picture and instructions below to learn how to practice this mudra.

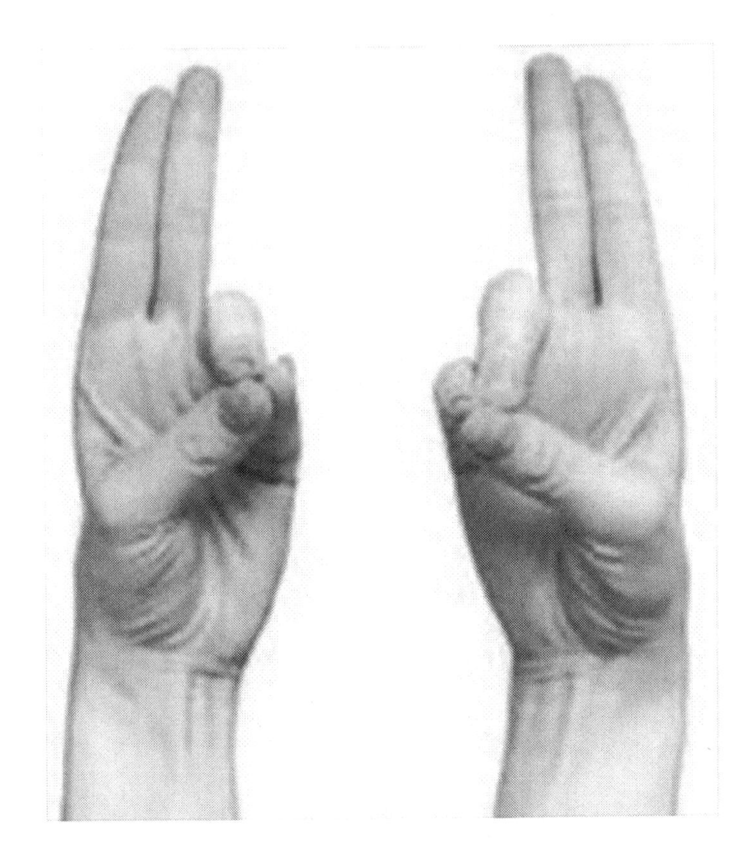

- When you get settled for meditation in your comfortable position, join your thumb little and ring finger together as you can see in the picture above and extend your index and middle finger outwards as shown in the picture.

- Then hold your hands either in a horizontal or vertical position.

- Keep holding the posture for at least 5 minutes or for the entire duration of your meditation session. Once you complete your session, you will notice that you feel energy running through your body that was not there when you started your session.

4. Lotus Mudra

Lotus mudra is a symbol of purity. In Buddhism, lotus position of hands is reserved to represent the opening of the heart. When you face rejection; you close your heart by slouching your shoulders and collapsing your chest. In other words, you make yourself unavailable to others when you're in stress which raises the tension between your peers and others close to you. As a result, you feel more stressed out when others neglect you because of your behavior.

By incorporating lotus mudra in your meditation, you open your heart to others and in return others return the favor and show gratitude to you, which ultimately reduces your stress levels and makes you happier than ever.

Use this mudra in cases where you find yourself in stressful situations because others are being rude to you. Given below are the instructions along with an image on how to perform this mudra.

- When you start your meditation session, join both hands in a way that your thumb meets your other thumb and your baby finger meets your other baby finger and both palms meet each other at the bottom. It will make a position of a flower in bloom.

- Hold this position throughout your session. You will feel a considerable change in the behavior of your peers and others close to you. When everybody is showing your gratitude, your mood will automatically lighten up and your stress levels go down.

Practice all the mentioned tips and tricks to enhance the effectiveness of your meditation sessions. Whichever route you take to fight your stress and anxiety, just remember one thing- change occurs with time but staying persistent is the key to accomplish and enjoy those changes and turn those temporary changes into everlasting ones. Therefore, keep fighting your stress through practicing meditation regularly and you will ultimately defeat your stress to live a happy and peaceful life.

Chapter Ten: Understanding your chakras

I feel that it is important that you are aware of the chakras or energy points in your body as you go through the process of learning to meditate. This helps you to recognize where the blockages are within your energy system and help you to become aware of what you need to work on to help to unblock those channels of energy during your meditation session. Let's start by explaining where the chakras are.

These are located in the points shown on the image and each one of them represents an area of your life and have specific names. If you look at the layout, this shows you why it's important to respect your posture when you meditate and at all other times, because the chakras are placed along the spine and if you are huddled or not sitting correctly, you are likely to block the energy in a certain chakra, causing effects like aches and pains or even emotional blockages.

The idea of meditation is to try and open the third eye chakra and experience enlightenment although this takes many years for some people to experience. Let's show you the names of the chakras and explain a little about the function and relevance of each of them so that you understand your inner self a little better. This helps you with your meditation because you can relate all of the pain you feel in life with the position of the chakra and thus get a good picture of why certain pains occur and what you can do about them.

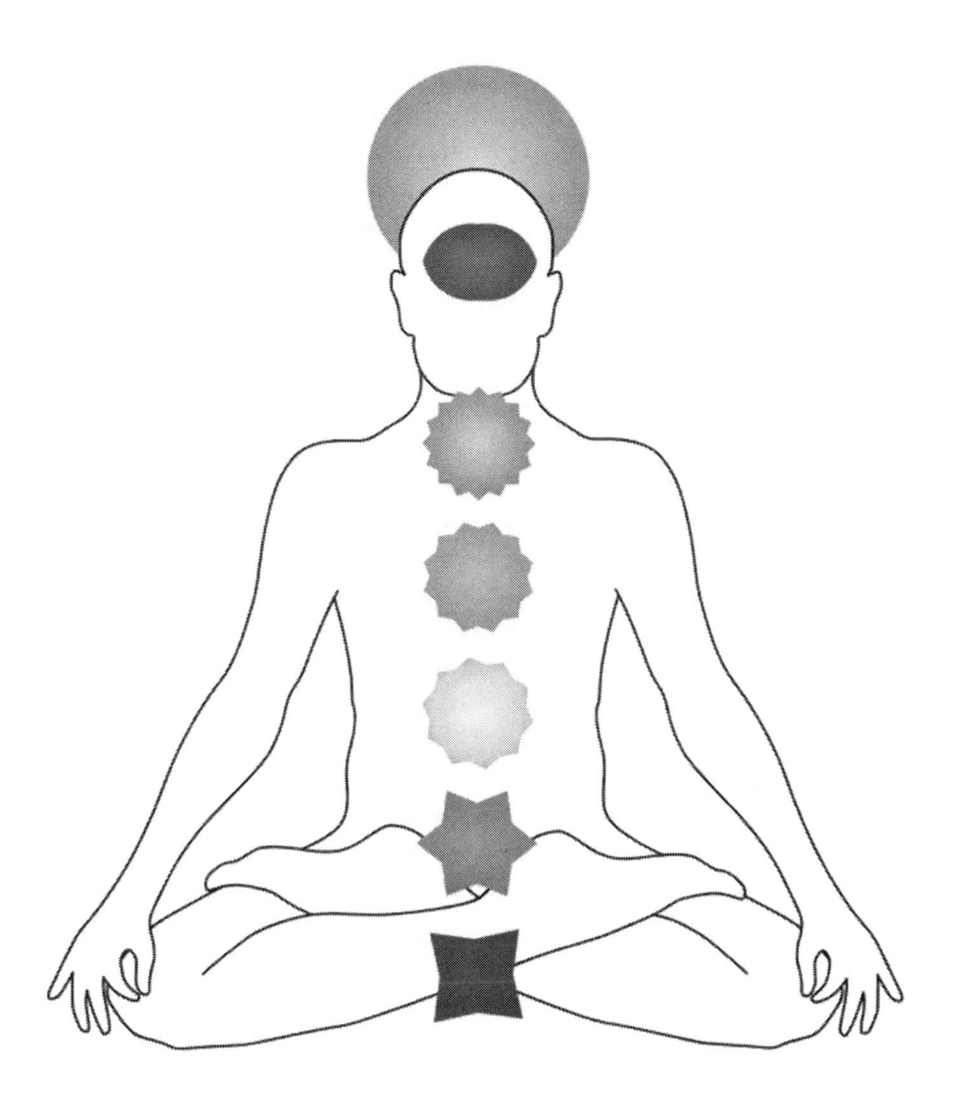

The **root chakra** is located at the base of the spine and from here that you gain your sense of ability to provide for yourself. This dictates your financial situation and the problems you may have been able to settle and find that security that every man needs. If you have problems in this area of the body, then there are things that you can do to improve your situation. The root chakra is all about feeling secure and grounded and during meditation is the reason that you place your feet flat on the ground if you are sitting on a chair. To heal this chakra, it would help to go barefoot sometimes and feel that connection between the earth and yourself. Maybe you have been wearing shoes that lift you from the ground and letting your feet feel their natural pose against the earth can indeed help to make you feel more grounded which is always going to help your meditation practice.

The next chakra upward is the **sacral chakra**, which you will find located a couple of inches below the navel. You need to think of this as aligned with your root chakra but a little further into the body. This is a pleasure center. When you enjoy your food, you please this area. When you feel a true abundance of your life, you can thank this chakra. However, when you feel deprived or unhappy, it may just be that this chakra is out of alignment and there are things that you can do to help it before your meditation session. Pelvic exercises can help this area of your body and dancing is one of the exercises that you can do to help your wellbeing and make this chakra ready for meditation. If it is out of alignment, you are likely to feel that you are unhappy and unsatisfied with life.

The third chakra from the base is the **Solar Plexus chakra**. This is found in the region around your tummy or upper abdomen area. Remember when we were doing the breathing exercises, these are great for this area of the body since you are allowing airflow to penetrate deep into your body and help the distribution of oxygen to all of the places that may otherwise have been deprived of it. Since this chakra deals with the way you feel about yourself in the sense of self-esteem, it's important that you do the breathing exercises regularly and that you respect a healthy diet. This helps you to ensure that you feel good about life and gain confidence. Meditation will help you in this area as well as dancing. You may also settle this area of the well-known butterflies by drinking chamomile tea or eating something with a peppermint flavor. Thus, if nervous before meditation, drink a peppermint tea.

The **fourth chakra** that I want to explain is the Heart Chakra and I am sure you will realize where this is! This chakra decides your ability to love and to open your heart to the love of others. When you have bad situations in your life that cause self-esteem issues, such as a broken relationship or broken trust, you tend to clam up and close off this chakra because you don't want to be hurt anymore. That's actually a mistake because the heart chakra does need that positive energy in order that you can feel love and love others. Isolating it purposely by cutting yourself off from others doesn't help the energy flow at all and your meditation practice will help because you will learn to first love yourself for who you are and to accept yourself. You also learn the things that you cannot change and learn to love the moment that you are in, rather than always looking backward toward the disappointments of your life. Love starts from within, from this moment, and can sustain you through all kinds of experiences within your life, so it is in your interests to keep your heart open to possibility, rather than closing it off as the result of hurt. Remember above all that everything changes from one moment to the next and that the only minute that actually matters is the NOW. Step into it and free this chakra to feel love and to give it. The area of meditation that helps you with healing this chakra is the ability to observe without judgment and to be able to accept others for who they are as well as accepting self. Every act of love, no matter how small, helps to open up the heart chakra and to give with no expectation of return will open the chakra to positive energy.

The throat chakra is exactly where you would imagine it to be. This is the chakra that deals with communication. Often in a working environment, you find it hard to discuss certain things and lack communication skills. You may even find that at the end of a day's work, even in an environment that puts no physical strain on the body, the area that hurts you the most is the neck. This is because we all feel pain in this area when we are lacking in the ability to voice our opinion or unable to say the words that we want to say. Meditation helps you to feel more confident and sure of yourself and also gives your mind the kind of clarity it needs in order to be able to communicate effectively. The best exercise for this chakra isn't talking. It's actually singing. Thus if you find yourself suffering from neck ache on a regular basis, start to take the world a little less seriously and sing. It doesn't matter if your voice is untrained or not very good. The release that you will feel from this exercise is worth it. It is allowing you to express yourself.

We already mentioned the third eye chakra and it is this that opens up to give you the bigger picture of life. When Siddhartha Gautama went out into the wilderness to find out all about why mankind suffers and what can be done about it, he experienced something that is called enlightenment. This means the opening up of all understanding or what Buddhists call Nirvana. The third eye allows you to use your intuition and to trust it. It allows you knowledge and when you meditate, this is the state of mind that you are aiming for though not everyone will reach that special place of understanding. You will learn more about yourself. You will be able to relate in a better way to the world around you through the process of meditation. However, to gain this real understanding of everything takes an awful lot of work. Eye exercises can help as can the Child's pose in yoga and meditation itself is a great exercise for this chakra which is why the end result of meditation is clarity, as explained in previous chapters. This chakra is located between the two eyes and when blocked, you may find that you don't relate to the world or are at loggerheads with your decision making processes.

The crown chakra – Even if you knew nothing about chakras, the position of this chakra is pretty obvious as it is where you would place a crown. This chakra is quite important. It's not about logic. It's a spiritual connection. When your mind is too busy to allow the crown chakra to work and to see the wonders of what's happening in the world around you, meditation will help. It will also help to be aware of the kinds of places that inspire you. For example, walking across a beach at sunset or sunrise can be uplifting. If you have a favorite place that makes you feel closer to your God or that makes you feel that you are part of a wonderful universe, then this helps to feed the crown chakra. Make sure that you have plenty of time surrounded by nature at its best.

Take walks, kick the autumn leaves, notice the new buds on the trees in spring and even make a snow angel for fun and just to be close to the wonder of the snow in winter. It's all about feeling a nearness to the creation and when you lack that in your life, your spirituality is lacking too. You see life in monochrome instead of seeing the full picture.

You can see from this chapter that your chakras have a lot to do with how you feel and can affect the efficiency of your meditation. Thus trying to make sure that you look after your chakras is very important. Posture, exercises, contact with the world and the feeling of love and empathy can all enhance the actions of your chakras. When you feel positive about the world in which you live, you will find that your chakras will align better and will help you to be able to meditate without any kind of problem getting in the way. When they are not aligned, you may find that your concentration is off, that you think too many negative thoughts or that you don't feel any sense of belonging or grounding. Thus, keeping them aligned is quite important to the process of meditation.

Chapter Eleven: Commonly asked questions about meditation

As this book is written for beginners, I want you to know the answers to commonly asked questions about meditation as these may also help you to meditate successfully and may answer any queries that you have following reading this book.

Is it better to meditate alone or in a group?

Both can be beneficial. The reason why meditating alone benefits you is because there are no distractions which we have already explained in the book. However, if you are not motivated to meditate, being in a group setting may help you because you will be with like-minded people who are also trying to find their way. You will also have a teacher who will be able to help you with areas of difficulty. Either can help. It's really up to you as an individual which path you choose to follow.

Is it okay to miss off a few days now and then?

Even when you are away on vacation, finding the time to meditate is the promise that you made to yourself when you started this voyage. It isn't to your benefit to mess around with your times or to leave meditation when you don't feel like it. It is a habit and you need to do it every single day if you want that habit to realistically help you to balance your life. If you need to adjust the time on the odd occasion, that's understandable, but you should still try to meditate on a daily basis.

Does it matter where you meditate?

When you have a little more experience of meditation, no, it doesn't matter. However, as a beginner, you should always choose a place where distractions are limited because your mind is not yet trained to meditate and you may find that your thought processes can't stop if you surround yourself with people. Thus, I would say from a beginner's point of view, and you should be in a calm environment. However, when you do gain experience, you may be able to meditate even sitting on a crowded airplane or waiting for a train. It's really a case of attuning your mind to the process of meditation and being able to breathe correctly.

There is one type of meditation which is very useful when you are in the work environment or when you simply want to step out of your busy schedule for a moment to re-energize. This type of meditation is walking meditation and while you do this you look down at your feet and as you breathe inward, you lift your foot from the ground, as you breathe out, move your foot forward and make sure that all of your senses are concentrating on the movement of the foot and the way that you are breathing. This is all about dropping all the worries of the world and simply breathing in motion with your movements – which is basically what yoga is all about – and if you do this in a quiet area, you will find that you will be able to approach your work in a better way afterward because you will have new energy to tackle the job that lies ahead.

Are there other breathing methods you can use to help you in your training?

There are several that you may wish to study once you have learned meditation. However, there is only one that I would suggest to beginners that will help you to gain energy and this can be done at any time of day to help you to energize your mind and give you stamina. In this system of breathing you breathe through alternate nostrils. This is called Nadi shodhan pranayama and is a type of breathing that you may be taught in a yoga class. To do this, you place your thumb over your right nostril and breathe in through the left nostril. Then move your thumb over to your left nostril and breathe out of the right nostril.

This kind of breathing can help you to relax when you are in an environment that is toxic in some way. Perhaps you have been in an argument and wanted to step aside and rethink things. Perhaps you simply want to straighten out your mind when you have been hyperactive or multi-tasking at work. Perhaps you are simply tired and overwhelmed by life. There are several YouTube videos on this type of breathing and it can help you in addition to your meditation practice. It helps to make you feel more energetic about life and happier in you.

There are several precautions to be taken when you attempt this kind of breathing. Keep your breathing natural and don't exaggerate the action of breathing. It's not about how much or how long you breathe in and out. It's merely a relaxing exercise so keep it that way. Try to avoid breathing via the mouth as this is a bad habit anyway which can result in swallowing air. Just as in meditation, your exhale should always be longer than your inhale and if you find it difficult to do this kind of breathing, you may be taking in too much oxygen and should lengthen the outward breath. Your thumb against your nostril should merely be a gentle hold rather than a push and you can place your fingers on your forehead as you do this which makes the hand position more comfortable.

Can you fail when you meditate?

There is no such thing as failure when you meditate. You can either find that you gain from the experience or at least gain insight as to what you need to change to make your next session more in keeping with what meditation is all about. The most common denominator is that people find it very hard to drop thoughts or to focus on the process of meditation. Since your mind is always working, then this is hardly a surprise. However, when you do manage to let go of thoughts and learn not to judge thoughts as they happen, this makes you much more compassionate and you will begin to find that you practice this compassion in your life. You may even surprise yourself. It's all good. By creating the habit of meditation, you will have days that you see as unproductive, but you will also go through the highs of realizing that you actually managed to meditate and did not let thoughts get in the way of the process. You cannot fail. You should not have to prove anything to yourself or others, but should merely place yourself in the moment and that's all there is to it. You need to be in the breath and in the moment, rather than looking back at your mistakes and capitalizing on them. It's all about this moment in time and as the moments pass, you are able to change your approach so that you feel more accomplished at the end of your meditation. However, when thoughts come, don't beat yourself up for it because it's what your mind is accustomed to and it will take a little time to change the way your mind operates.

What's the best feeling you can have after meditation?

I have asked many students this and the answers I get vary, although what seems to be a universal answer is the feeling of clarity and peace. People say that they feel comfort from meditation that they don't get from any other action and that the peace encompasses their whole being and places them into the moment. They also explain that it's like putting down a heavy load and replacing it with something so light that it's no burden at all to carry it – the feeling of self. It's unlike memories or feelings you get from a one off act of kindness. It's a feeling of completeness and that's the best way to describe it. If you carry on with your daily meditation, you may find that your description of it is slightly different, but you need to remember, you are not trying to attain anyone else's idea of Nirvana. You are trying to experience it for yourself. The peace that you get from being in the moment and giving no credence to past or future is amazing.

Conclusion

Congratulations on finishing this book! I have been practicing meditation for a long time and based on my experience; I made every effort to help you understand meditation better so that you can experience transformational benefits of it.

I believe this book shared you all the necessary information you needed to understand meditation better and apply it to your life in order to be happy and relieve stress and anxiety forever.

The next step is to implement what you have learned.

Made in the USA
Middletown, DE
09 February 2019